TRAVEL SERVICES
Give your holiday a smoother start

e issue of all cards are subject to the Bank's assessment of your financial status and you must be 18 or over to apply. Lloyds Bank Plc is a member of IMRO and of the Banking Ombudsman Scheme.

There was no mad rush. Everybody has a guaranteed seat.

Out over the Channel you can see

Watch seagulls fly backwards.

a kittiwake winging its way backwards back to Dover.

Funny. You don't feel as though you're going fast.

In fact you're going at a real rate of knots on the world's largest catamaran.

Soon you'll be on the road again.

Driving down poplar-lined avenues on your way through France.

Before then there's just enough time to have a stroll out on deck and a coffee at the bar.

Only just though.

Like the Hovercraft, the SeaCat speeds you across to Calais or Boulogne far quicker than a conventional ferry.

Cross the Channel with Hoverspeed and you'll be able to watch a few of those going backwards as well.

DOVER · CALAIS · BOULOGNE
FOLKESTONE · BOULOGNE

CONTACT YOUR TRAVEL AGENT FOR RESERVATIONS OR INFORMATION. OR CALL HOVERSPEED ON DOVER (0304) 240241.

DRIVING IN
EUROPE

Kogan Page Limited
120 Pentonville Road
London N1 9JN

© Gordon Cole, 1992

**British Library Cataloguing in Publication
Data**

A CIP record for this book is available from
the British Library.

ISBN 0 7494 0259 8

Typeset by DP Photosetting, Aylesbury, Bucks
Printed in Slovenia by Gorenjski Tisk

DRIVING IN EUROPE

Gordon Cole

KOGAN
PAGE

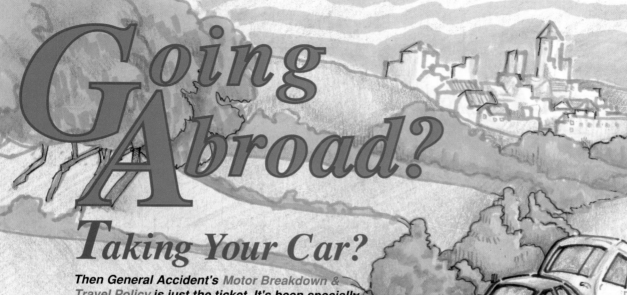

Going Abroad?

Taking Your Car?

Then General Accident's *Motor Breakdown & Travel Policy* **is just the ticket.** It's been specially designed for driving holidays to protect your car, your family and your belongings whilst abroad.

And make sure you take a green card with you, to extend your comprehensive motor insurance to most EC countries. Don't assume your existing insurance will apply.

For more details, visit your local General Accident office or your insurance adviser.

And once you're home again, remember - General Accident has a full range of policies designed to meet most of your insurance requirements.

General Accident

CONTENTS

FOREWORD

At long last, the book I have been waiting for. As the Chief Examiner of the Institute of Advanced Motorists, I receive many requests for information on driving on the Continent, with questions such as 'What is it like to drive on the "wrong" side of the road?' 'Are their motorways dangerous?' 'What happens if I break down?' 'How do I deal with foreign road signs?'

All these answers are to be found in this excellent new guide. I feel that the text coupled with the superb photographs will certainly make driving abroad more enjoyable.

Ted Clements MBE
Chief Examiner
Institute of Advanced
Motorists

ACKNOWLEDGEMENTS

A special thank you to the people of Europe, who unwittingly made the content of some of the pictures more realistic for me.

Many thanks to Vauxhall Motors Ltd who so kindly supplied the vehicles.

All films developed by Kenton Photographic Colour Laboratories Ltd (Tel: 081-206 0226).

All photographs taken by the author using LEICA cameras and lenses.

The photographs in this book were taken by the author at different times of the day and in different seasons, using the natural light available at the time. The intention is to give the reader an insight into the many different light, colour and weather conditions that can be expected when driving in Europe.

PREFACE

Although there is a lot of pleasure to be gained from driving in Europe, many people have been deterred from doing so in the past. Today, the European Community's (EC's) 'People's Europe' programme enables the freedom of movement between member states. Providing drivers observe the requirements of the country being visited (ie they have full driving licence and are properly insured), they can enjoy the run of Europe.

More and more people are choosing the freedom of an independent holiday. They find that the ease of travel and the way of life they experience are more interesting and enjoyable than taking a package holiday. Yet people are still discouraged by quite superficial problems, such as the language, road signs, or (most daunting of all!) driving on the 'wrong' side of the road.

Driving in Europe will do away with all these fears. It shows clearly the correct driving procedures for a huge number of different situations, and will ensure that motoring on the Continent is enjoyable and risk-free.

Wouldn't you rather be insured with a company who really knows Europe?

With over 20,000 staff in 17 European countries, Zurich is one of the continent's largest insurers.

As befitting our European heritage, all our UK private car policies offer a free green card for up to 45 days holiday motoring. Indeed, our Zurich Fifty PLUS policy **automatically** provides a Continental Assistance package including accident and breakdown recovery and medical expenses cover up to £100,000, so there's no need to buy additional cover for your journey.

It's also a comforting thought to know that, in most European countries , there's a Zurich office to assist you.

So if you travel to Europe with your car, please ask your insurance advisor for details of Zurich and our policies.

ZURICH
I N S U R A N C E

Offices throughout Europe

PLANNING YOUR JOURNEY

Once you have decided on the type of holiday you want and the countries you are going to visit, you need to plan your route carefully and check if any visas are needed. No visas are required for countries within the EC, but if you are in doubt, you should contact the relevant country's tourist office. There is a list of addresses and telephone numbers at the back of this book.

You will, of course, need some appropriate currency. If you are travelling through more than one country, make sure you have about £20 worth of the currency of each country through which you will pass. This could prove invaluable in an emergency.

Think carefully about what type of holiday is most suitable for you. Some people opt for a cycling holiday, some travel by motorbike or with a caravan, and there are even people who prefer to take a chance and hitchhike their way around Europe. The car, however, is certainly the most popular means of transport.

If you are staying in a hotel or camping site for the first night of your holiday, find out how to get there, and plan your driving time and route well before you set off. This will save you a lot of trouble on your first day, and allow you to really enjoy your holiday from the outset.

Planning your route is not as hard as people think. A good map is,

obviously, essential, and there is a list of recommended maps and guides at the back of this book. Alternatively, the Royal Automobile Club (RAC) or the Automobile Association (AA) can plan your route for you. They will supply a computerised chart giving simple-to-follow directions to and from your destination. There is, however, a charge for this service.

Ask yourself how far you intend to travel on the first day, and what kind of roads you wish to use. If you use 'A' or 'B' roads, you will see more of the countryside, and be able to stop whenever you want. Remember that it is important to stop for regular breaks when driving for long distances so that you remain as alert as possible. The alternative is to use a motorway, which will, of course, save you time, but might prove expensive if there are a lot of tolls (see page 59). You will also miss seeing a lot of the countryside, and if you have young passengers in the vehicle, travelling for a long time on a motorway can be boring for them. It is hard to concentrate fully on the road with fidgeting children in the car.

COSTING YOUR HOLIDAY

The cost of your trip will be dictated by the kind of holiday you have chosen. For example, if you are camping or taking a caravan, the sites you stay at will almost certainly be cheaper than a hotel. How many people will there

be in the vehicle? How far do you intend to travel? Ask yourself all these questions when budgeting for your journey. If you get it wrong, remember, you could find yourself stranded miles from home, without any money!

The checklist below will help you work out your budget. Although no prices are given here, you can find further information on pages 15 and 42.

Passport

Have you got one? Is it valid?

Visa

Will you need one for the country you intend to visit? How much will it cost? (Contact the relevant tourist office for this information. They are listed on page 107.)

Ferry/tunnel

Find out how much this is going to cost. (Contact the ferry company you will be using and get a quote. Ferry companies are listed on page 108.)

Insurance

Check with your agent to make sure your vehicle, caravan and your personal insurance will provide adequate cover.

1 Preparing For Your Holiday

Fuel

Work out how many miles you are going to travel.

Hotels and camping sites

Find out the estimated cost (see the list of recommended travel guides on page 111).

Food

The cost of eating, of course, depends on you, but decide how much you want to spend, and budget accordingly. (Again, a good travel guide will give you an idea of the cost of both catering for yourself and of eating out.)

Tolls

The further you travel on motorways the more it will cost you. See the section on tolls (page 59) for more details.

Spending money

This will be determined by you of course, but remember: it is better to take too much than too little.

Exchange rate

You will not usually get pound-for-pound value on the exchange rate, and will often have to pay a small handling charge when you change money. Bear this in mind when costing your holiday, and, if you have time, shop around for the best rates. They are displayed in all high street banks. See the table of examples above.

EXCHANGE RATES

Country	Currency	To the pound
Austria	schilling	19.5
Belgium	francs	57.2
Denmark	kroner	10.9
Eire	punt	1
Finland	Finmark	7.7
France	francs	9.5
Germany	Deutchmarks	2.8
Greece	drachmas	325
Italy	lira	2,110
Luxembourg	francs	57.2
Netherlands	guilder	3.1
Norway	kroner	11
Portugal	escudos	243
Spain	pesetas	175
Sweden	krona	10.3
Switzerland	francs	2.5

Exchange rates are subject to daily changes, and this table gives only *very approximate* rates. You should check the up-to-the-minute exchange rates at your bank on the day you buy your currency.

BOOKING, TRAVEL AND FINANCIAL ARRANGEMENTS

When you have decided whereabouts on the Continent you wish to begin your holiday, you should think carefully about how you are going to get there. There are several options open to you: take your own car or caravan on the ferry (see pages 27–32), or else fly or sail over, and hire transport when you arrive (see below).

The Channel Tunnel

When the Channel Tunnel finally opens in 1993, your choice of how to get to your chosen destination will be even wider. The tunnel will offer an express rail service which will be able to carry five cars in each container unit. There will be toilet facilities on these trains but little else. Once in the container, there is nothing for you to do or see until you reach the terminal at the other end. It is estimated that the travelling time through the tunnel will be 35 minutes and payment for the journey will be made at a toll at the departure terminal.

Hiring transport

If you choose to fly or sail to your holiday destination with the intention of hiring a vehicle on arrival, it is advisable to book your vehicle in advance with the rental firm you have chosen. This is usually no more expensive than hiring on arrival and can also save you a lot of time and

trouble, especially if you arrive in the middle of the night!

When hiring a car or motorbike, you must have your driving licence with you (and an International Driving Permit (IDP) if applicable – see pages 20–21). Payment for rental will always be in advance. It will be charged by the day and will include a fee for insurance. Petrol is, of course, your cost. If you are considering hiring a motorbike, it is advisable to take your own safety helmet with you as helmets are not readily available for

A wide selection of motorcycles and mopeds to suit people with varying degrees of motorcycling experience can be seen at this typical hire centre in St Tropez.

hire in some countries. It would also be a risk to trust a hired helmet to provide the necessary protection in the event of an accident.

TAKE A BREATHER.

If you're travelling to France, Ireland or Holland, why not start your holiday before you arrive?

On Sealink's ships you'll enjoy the benefits brought by a £178 million investment in our services.

We now offer you a wider range of routes than any other ferry company and have opened our Southampton-Cherbourg crossing to smooth your passage to Western France.

You can even leave your complete holiday arrangements to us: anything from a short break to a fortnight's package.

It's one way of ensuring your stay is as enjoyable as the journey.

FOR DETAILS OF ALL OUR SERVICES,
CONTACT YOUR LOCAL TRAVEL AGENT OR MOTORING
ORGANISATION, OR CALL US ON 0233 647047.

SEALINK STENA LINE

Whatever mode of travel you decide on to get to the Continent, you will have to make a reservation. To do this, either contact the company operating the service you require, or book your reservation through a travel agent. Do not rely on making a last minute reservation; you could well be disappointed. All ferry companies and airlines offer guides detailing sailing times and dates, routes and tariffs, and you should look carefully at these before you set off. A list of ferry companies and other useful services is given at the back of the book.

Whatever country or countries you intend to visit you will need some ready cash in the relevant currency and a nominal sum of about £20 for each country you will be visiting is essential.

One of the safest and most convenient ways of carrying your holiday money is in the form of travellers' cheques. These can be replaced quickly if they are lost or stolen, and you can get them in many currencies from banks, building societies or travel agents. Expect to pay a small commission charge for the service, and allow at least three days between ordering and receiving them. When you collect the cheques, you will be given a leaflet telling you what to do in an emergency, and a form on which to note down the numbers of your cheques. it is essential that you keep these items separate from your travellers' cheques and in a safe place.

This hole-in-the-wall cash machine in Bruges can exchange ten different currencies into Belgian francs, twenty-four hours a day. There are similar cash machines throughout Europe.

Eurocheques and Eurocheque guarantee cards are available from banks, and are ideal for travellers who are not sure exactly how much money they will need. They are also a useful back-up if you run out of travellers' cheques, and are more widely accepted than most credit cards. There is, however, a small charge for the Eurocheque guarantee card, and a handling fee and commission on each cheque. Allow at least 14 days' notice when ordering these, to ensure you have them on time.

Chargecards, credit cards and some of the new payment cards can all be used to obtain money abroad. They are an easy way to pay for goods and services and to obtain local currency. Most plastic cards are based on one of the two big international payment systems, MasterCard (Access) and Visa, both of which are accepted all over the world. While most places accept both types of card, some only accept one or the other, and it is a good idea to take both a MasterCard and a Visa card. Payment (or debit) cards look like credit cards but act like cheques. They allow you to buy goods and services and then automatically debit your current account. Unlike a cheque there is no separate guarantee card and no fixed £50, £100 or £250 spending limit. Examples of these include the Lloyds Bank Payment Card and Barclays Connect Card, both of which can be used widely abroad. Credit cards can be used to get local currency from hole-in-the-wall cash machines in about 40 different countries. Acceptability varies from country to country, so don't rely on these as your main source of cash!

Weigh up the pros and cons of each of the above options well before you begin your holiday, but bear in mind that it is prudent to take at least one credit card in case of an emergency. Remember to take some sterling as well for snacks on the ferry etc. Finally, with all the different currencies used in Europe, and the often confusing exchange rates, it is well worth taking a pocket calculator with you!

Your bank, building society or travel agent will be pleased to give you advice on your methods of payment abroad. Travellers' cheques are good if you are on a tight budget while credit cards give you more freedom to spend as you go, but could mean coming home to a large bill. A payment card, however, allows you to spend only what you have in your bank account and so limits your spending. Some countries are strict about how much local currency you may take in or bring out and some are less keen on accepting plastic cards than others. It is wise, therefore, to seek advice on these matters, depending on where you intend to travel.

DOCUMENTATION

There is a number of documents and certificates which you may be required to take with you on your holiday, and these are described below. Check carefully which you will need, and ensure you have them before you set off.

Driving licence
You must have a valid driving licence for the category of vehicle that you will be driving abroad. A provisional licence is *not* acceptable. If you are going to drive in EC countries and have a full British EC (pink) model licence, you can do so without an International Driving Permit (IDP). If you have a green driving licence, however, you should obtain an IDP. Regardless of the colour of your GB driving licence, you *must* take it with you. The minimum age to drive a motor car in most EC countries is 18.

International Driving Permit
If you intend to drive in countries that are not in the EC you will need an IDP. IDPs are issued by the Automobile Association (AA), Royal Automobile Club (RAC), Royal Scottish Automobile Club (RSAC) and the National Breakdown Recovery Club (NBRC) under authority delegated by the Secretary of State under Article 1 (8) of the Motor Vehicles (International Circulation) Order 1975. They are issued to any person who satisfies the requirements as regards minimum

age and competence to drive, whether or not that person is a member of the association. There is a nominal fee that has to be paid to the association issuing the permit.

Vehicle insurance

Amazingly, some motorists are prepared to cross the Channel without adequate vehicle insurance. It is of the utmost importance that you inform your motor insurance company or broker of your intention to take your car abroad, as you might not be insured to do so. Providing there is no reason for refusing your request, you will be issued with a green card. (Its official title is the International Motor Insurance Card or Carte Internationale D'Assurance Automobile.) The green card is an internationally recognised certificate of motor insurance. It provides proof that the driver has the minimum cover required by law to drive in the countries shown on the card. (A specimen green card is shown here.)

An international motor insurance card (green card).

*For details of Letter Code for Category of Vehicle, see middle page

1. INTERNATIONAL MOTOR INSURANCE CARD 2. ISSUED UNDER THE AUTHORITY OF MOTOR INSURER'S BUREAU

3. FROM **VALID** TO	4. Serial and Policy Number
Day Month Year Day Month Year	**GB/105/**
1st August 1991 5th August 1991	RMM 458890
(Both Dates Inclusive)	

5. Registration Number (or if none) Chassis or Engine Number	6. Category and make of Vehicle*
H183 DPP	A ASTRA

(Cancel Country inapplicable)   A   CH   B   D   DK   F   GB   I   IRL   L   NL

N   S   SF   ⊠G   CS   DDR   E   GR   H   ⊠   ⊠Q   ⊠   ⊠A   P   ⊠   ⊠   T   ⊠   U

7. Name and Address of Insured (or User of the Vehicle)

VAUXHALL & ASSOCIATED Co's
CENTRAL PARK, OHIO AVENUE
SALFORD QUAYS. MANCHESTER

8. This Card has been issued by: (Name and Address of Insurer)

Royal Insurance (UK) LTD
51 Clarendon Road
Watford
Hertfordshire WD1 1HU

9. Signature of Insurer

MANAGING DIRECTOR

ORIGINAL

INTERNATIONAL MOTOR INSURANCE CARD
CARTE INTERNATIONALE D'ASSURANCE AUTOMOBILE

(1)   In each country visited, the Bureau of that country assumes, in respect of the use of the vehicle referred to herein, the liability of an Insurer in accordance with the laws relating to compulsory insurance in that country.

(2)   After the date of expiry of this Card, liability is assumed by the Bureau of the country visited, if so required by the law of such country or by any agreement with its Government. In such case, the within–mentioned insured undertakes to pay the premium due for the duration of the stay after the date for which the Insurance Card is valid has passed.

(3)   I, the within–mentioned Insured, hereby authorise the Motor Insurers' Bureau and the Bureaux of any mentioned countries,to which it may delegate such powers, to accept service of legal proceedings, to handle and eventually settle, on my behalf, any claim for damages in respect of liability to third parties required to be covered under the compulsory insurance laws of the country or countries specified herein, which may arise from the use of the vehicle in that country (those countries).

Personal insurance

Every year thousands of British holidaymakers are treated in hospitals abroad, or lose or have valuable possessions stolen. Should your vehicle become unusable because of an accident, breakdown, fire or theft, you will need the best assistance possible. It is therefore essential to take out personal, as well as vehicle insurance.

There are so many different policies available you will have to shop around to find the best one for your requirements. You can get medical treatment within the EC, but you will need to get a form E111 and leaflet T1, both of which are available from post offices. Sometimes treatment is free, but you will often have to pay part of the cost yourself. All the major insurance companies offer numerous types of travel insurance so ring around for quotes and compare the benefits before you make a choice.

Bail bond

Should you be unfortunate enough to be involved in a traffic accident in Spain, the consequences could be very serious. The vehicle may be impounded and the driver detained pending trial. A bail bond is a guarantee of bail payment, as stated on the bond, and of release of the vehicle and the driver. If you are planning on going to Spain, therefore, contact your motor insurance broker for details and issue of the bond.

International Camping Carnet

The International Camping Carnet (ICC) is an official document for campers which is accepted as proof of identity in lieu of a passport at most camping and caravanning sites in Europe. Holders of the carnet are given a discount on the advertised charges at some sites. It also provides third party insurance cover up to a stated amount while camping abroad. The carnet is compulsory on some sites and in some countries. For details of the carnet, and its cost, contact The Caravan Club (see Useful Addresses).

Passport

You must have a valid passport to travel abroad if you are 16 or over. Younger children may travel on a parent's passport, and if you already have a family passport which includes the particulars of your wife or husband, it is still valid until its expiry date. To apply for a passport you need the form 'United Kingdom Passport Application' which is available from any main post office. Although there are numerous questions to be answered, the form is self-explanatory, and as long as you read the questions carefully, you should not have any problems filling it in. Remember, though, that it is a serious offence to give false information on your passport. It is strongly advised that you make your passport application *at least* six weeks before you need it.

Visa

You do not require a visa to drive through or visit any country in the EC. If you are planning to travel outside the EC, ask at the relevant embassy or tourist office if a visa is required.

Log book

You must take the original vehicle registration document with you when going abroad. If you are going to drive a borrowed vehicle, the registration document must be accompanied by a letter of authority from the registered owner. If a UK-registered hired or leased vehicle is to be driven abroad, the vehicle registration document will normally be retained by the leasing/hiring company. You must, therefore, ask for a vehicle certificate as authorisation for you to take and drive their vehicle abroad.

Vehicle excise licence (road tax)

You must have a valid vehicle excise licence displayed on the windscreen of your car all the time that you are abroad.

Certificate of roadworthiness

If the vehicle to be taken abroad is three years old or more, you must have an MOT certificate which is valid for all the time you are abroad.

GB plate

It is compulsory to display a GB plate on the rear of your vehicle, caravan, trailer or boat while driving abroad. The GB plate must be of the authorised size, design, shape and colour, and can be obtained from ferry companies, motoring organisations and accessory shops.

Ferry tickets

It is surprising how many people actually forget to take their ferry tickets with them when they leave home! Check to make sure you have packed all your essential documents before you set off.

Boats and boat engines

If you are considering taking a boat (with or without an engine) to Europe, you should first contact the Royal Yachting Association (see Useful Addresses). They will help you with all the documentation that is required in the various countries.

A final point, and one that is often forgotten, is the condition of the vehicle itself. When was it last serviced? Is it due for another service soon? It is important that you have the vehicle checked about a week before you start your journey; it doesn't take long, and it makes good motoring sense.

LOADING THE VEHICLE

It's all too easy, when going on holiday, to pack a car load of useless items and leave things that you might actually need at home. Before you even begin to pack, make a list of essential items. Then stick to that list! Extras can be added later, if there is any space left for them.

The way a vehicle is loaded is important for both comfort and safety reasons. At any ferry port you can see numerous overloaded cars, with the load badly distributed. Often, all the heaviest items of luggage have been loaded on one side, and, to make matters worse, the heaviest passenger sits on that same side! Consequently, the stability and handling are severely impaired, and the vehicle is potentially dangerous. The correct distribution of weight is very important. The heaviest suitcase should be placed at the front of the luggage compartment, so it is lodged against the middle of the rear seat. Smaller, lighter, items of luggage can be put either side of the first suitcase. Should there be two heavy suitcases, they should be put one on top of the other, or, if the luggage compartment is not deep enough, placed one beside the other. Smaller items of luggage can be packed either side, preventing heavy cases moving from side to side.

Caravans

If you are taking a caravan abroad, figure 1 shows how best to load it for safe and easy handling while towing. A badly loaded caravan could be very unstable and prove extremely dangerous on the road. The basic principles of loading that apply to cars and other vehicles also apply to caravans.

THE VEHICLE EMERGENCY PACK

A vehicle emergency pack contains tools and replacement items that could be invaluable should you break down, particularly if you do not have easy access to a garage. It is prudent to take an emergency pack with you whenever you drive abroad. Some of the items are in fact compulsory on the Continent; caravans, for example, are required by law to carry a fire extinguisher in many countries.

Most vehicle manufacturers offer vehicle emergency packs for hire, and these are available from main dealer networks. The cost of their hire is usually very modest, and you will be invoiced only for what has been used from the pack. You can also hire the packs from motoring organisations, like the AA and RAC. (These organisations also hire out many other accessories, such as ski racks, bike racks, roof racks and surfboard carriers.)

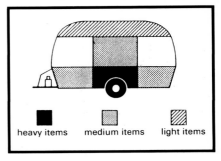

Figure 1 *Sensible loading*

heavy items   medium items   light items

The emergency pack contains:

- First aid kit
- Fire extinguisher
- Spare bulbs
- Jump-start leads
- Plastic tape
- Set of spark plugs
- Selection of tools
- Work light (12 volt)
- Side window repair kit
- Warning triangle
- Mirror repair kit
- Yellow reflective jacket
- Tow rope

The warning triangle, first aid kit, fire extinguisher and spare bulbs are compulsory in some countries, but it is strongly recommended that you carry these items in all countries.

The vehicle emergency pack.

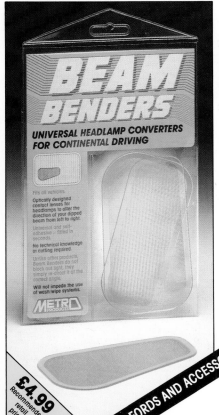

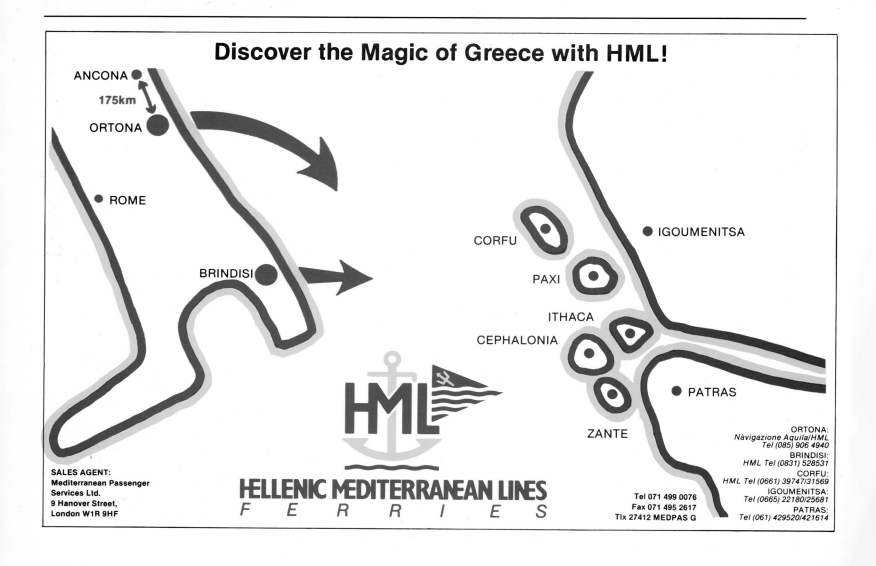

ARRIVING AT THE PORT

Once you have received your travel tickets you will be given your check-in and sailing times. It is essential that vehicles and foot passengers alike arrive at the port *at least* one hour before their scheduled sailing time, as the company reserves the right to alter sailing times without prior notice, and ships may sail up to fifteen minutes before they are scheduled to do so.

As you enter the port, signs will direct you to the departure area and ticket control. Here you will be met by officials from your ferry company, who will ask to see your tickets. Once these have been checked they will be returned to you, minus the outgoing ticket. A small sticker will be placed on your windscreen, informing other officials in the port that you have passed through ticket control. Next, you will be directed to passport control and Customs and you should have your passport available for inspection. From the passport office you should proceed to the embarkation lanes, where you may have to wait a short while before boarding the ferry.

Numerous shipping companies and motoring organisations have offices at the port, and they will be able to give you any information which you may need for your journey. You can also make any necessary last minute purchases, and perhaps collect your vehicle emergency pack. (Remember to leave room in the car for this!) If

When your ticket has been checked, you will be directed to passport control and Customs.

This sign on the quayside shows sailing and loading times, destinations and shipping company names.

A marshall will direct you on to the upper or lower car deck of the ferry.

2 Crossing the Channel

you do decide to make use of the shops or restaurants at the port, take care not to leave your car unattended for too long. You may find you are obstructing other travellers trying to board the ferry.

Board the ferry when you are told to do so.

BOARDING THE FERRY

Once you are on the car deck you will be guided to where you should park your vehicle. Park as usual, but slip into first gear. If the sea is choppy this will back the handbrake up. Check before you open your door, as car decks are always crowded, and you do not want to hit anyone. Before you leave your car, it is sensible to make a note of its whereabouts on the car deck. Make sure you take with you everything you will need as you will not be able to return to your car during the crossing. Then make your way up to the passenger deck.

If you are disabled or have a disabled passenger, contact the marshall at the loading point on the quayside. He will make arrangements for you to park close to a lift, and provide a wheelchair if necessary. Most ferry companies now have special facilities for the disabled, and on the newest ships many cabins, lounges, bars, shops, bureaux de change, restaurants and toilets are

There are plenty of restaurants and other facilities on board the ferry.

Ah! to B&Ireland
(at the end of a perfect day)

We're the Irish owned travel company that offers convenient comfortable and competitively priced ferry routes from Holyhead to the heart of Dublin and from Pembroke to Rosslare.

B&I offers great family value saving pounds on fares and on board in our duty free shops and restaurants. We also have the most extensive range of inclusive holidays in Ireland by both sea and air.

Get the B&I Holidays in Ireland brochure now by calling 051-236 8325.

Holiday B&Ireland
THE IRISH EXPERTS

**HOLYHEAD – DUBLIN
PEMBROKE – ROSSLARE**

B&I LINE

wheelchair-accessible. It is helpful to tell your travel agent or ferry company if any passengers travelling with you are disabled when you make your ferry reservation.

Safety regulations

The following information is issued by ferry companies. The guidelines must be complied with; they are there for your own safety and the safety of other passengers.

- Access to the car deck is forbidden during the crossing, so make sure you take everything you need on the passenger decks with you – especially your vehicle keys, tickets and passport(s).

- Lock up your vehicle and leave it in gear with the handbrake on.

- Cars powered by LPG should have tanks switched off when on the vehicle decks.

- Do not carry petrol cans on board – full or empty. Do not overfill your tank.

- Loose gas cylinders must not be carried. Make sure gas cylinders, cookers and fridges in caravans are properly switched off.

- Do not smoke on the vehicle decks.

- Pay attention to safety announcements on board and familiarise yourself with the emergency notices. These are posted at muster stations in the main passenger areas.

- Do not block access to the safety equipment or passenger escapes.

Make sure you read the emergency notices in the main passenger areas.

On board the ferry

The amount of time you spend on the ferry will, of course, depend on the length of your journey. The crossing from Dover to Calais, for example, takes between 70 and 90 minutes, while it takes about 9½ hours to sail from Harwich to the Hook of Holland.

There is a wide variety of facilities to keep travellers occupied on the ferry. For the children, there are play areas, crêches, child minders, video games and other entertainments. For adults there are shops (including duty free shops), a choice of restaurants, cinemas, discos and bars. (Bear in mind, though, that drinking and driving laws apply in all the EC countries, so drivers should stick to soft drinks.) For a good night's sleep, or even just a little peace and quiet, cabins are often well worth paying a little extra for.

View from the bridge of a ferry that is about to dock in Cherbourg, France.

LEAVING THE FERRY

Many passengers like to stand on the decks of the ferry and try to spot the coastline of their destination. When they see land, some people think it is time to return to their cars, but the distance is deceptive. Wait on the passenger deck until you hear an announcement telling you to return to the car deck.

If you took note of where and on what car deck you left your vehicle, go straight there. If you were less organised and failed to do so, one of the deck hands should be able to help you. The deck will, once again, be very crowded, so watch out for car doors being opened, etc.

Do not start your engine until you are told to do so by one of the marshalls, and make sure that seat belts are fastened and children are properly restrained. The law regarding seat belts in the UK applies in all other EC countries too. You will soon be directed off the car deck and onto the connecting bridge to the quayside. You will then be on the Continent!

Vehicles leaving a ferry.

Relax your way across the Channel.

Imagine a ferry where you didn't have to battle to get on board. Where you could sit down to a choice of inviting meals without having to rush. Where you actually had time to browse around the Duty Free shops.   In fact where the crossing was like a holiday in itself.

Take it easy

Modern, spacious ships with a choice of bars and restaurants offer the ideal environment in which to eat and relax.
Our Duty Free shops spoil you for choice. And we even keep the children occupied as the miles pass gently by.
So once in France, we deliver the whole family refreshed and ready for the open motorways of Europe.

The more convenient way

Our ships slip quietly out of Ramsgate en-route to Dunkerque five times a day. (Ramsgate is no further from London than Dover and easily reached via the M2).

For more information call
0843 595522
or ask your travel agent.

BOULOGNE SUR MER: SEA AND HISTORY
THE CITY OF THE SEA

NAUSICAA:

Boulogne's sea centre is designed to be a veritable initiation course: within the centre you may dive in the plankton, discover marine life in cold seas, find yourself in a tropical lagoon, observe the behaviour of different species of fish, dive to a depth of 3000 metres, experience tuna fishing and life aboard a fishing trawler, watch a shoal of sharks swimming alongside you, tickle a skate, manage the sea's resources and be present at testing in the research area.

Practical information:

ENTRY: Adults: 45,00 Frs
Children: 30,00 Frs
Group fees (minimum 20 persons) upon request.

OPENING TIMES: April to September:
from 10 a.m. to 8 p.m.
October to March:
from 10 a.m. to 6 p.m.

FACILITIES: restaurant (seats 300) – gift shop – bookshop – swimming pool – car park (350 spaces) – bus (25 seats).

FOR FURTHER INFORMATION AND BOOKINGS:

NAUSICAA – Centre National de la Mer –
Boulevard Ste Beuve
62200 BOULOGNE SUR MER
Tél: 21.30.98.98   Fax: 21.30.93.94

SEA-ANGLING:

Boulogne Sur Mer offers sea angling excursions for beginners and experienced fishermen alike. Equipment may be hired on board.

FOR FURTHER INFORMATION AND BOOKINGS:

LES ARSOUINS
19 Square de la mutualité
62200 BOULOGNE SUR MER
Tél: 21.87.55.99

FISHING CLUB BOULONNAIS
3 rue Coquelin
62200 BOULOGNE SUR MER
Tél: 21.31.94.10

GASTRONOMY:

Boulogne Sur Mer is France's first fishing port; come and discover its gastronomic riches, in particular "La Gainée", a sort of fish stew which uses 3 different types of fish, this is a speciality of Boulogne and is served in many of the town's restaurants.

TOWN OF ART AND HISTORY THE OLD TOWN:

Presents the best preserved fortified development in the North of France and dates back to the beginning of the XIIIth Century. The old town is recognised as

being a site of great cultural value and hosts a yearly event known as "Mausic et Remparts", this takes place in June and is rapidly gaining in popularity amongst music lovers and becoming more devoted to the best known British musicians. In July-August, visitors are invited to experience the excitement of the town's past through various forms of street entertainment and the presentation of historical scenes.

SUIVEZ LE CYGNE:

You may "follow the swan" (Boulogne's coat of arms) on one or both of two trails starting at any one of the gateways to the old town. Follow the signs on the yellow route and you will visit the main monuments, the chateau museum, the cathedral, the belfry, the annonciade couvent . . .
Follow the green signs and you will discover the fortified town.

GUIDED TOURS:

Available for individuals and groups who will be accompanied by guides registered with La Caisse Nationale des Monuments Historiques (National Trust for Historical Monuments). Tél: 21.80.56.78

THE CHATEAU MUSEUM:

This is the masterpiece of the old town. Having fulfilled its defensive role through the centuries, the Chateau of the Counts of

Boulogne now houses the magnificent museum collection in 4000 m2. From the vaulted rooms to the underground passages and the attic which was converted in the XVIIIth Century, the amazed visitor will pass from the discovery of ancient Egypt and her gods to the most fascinating collection of Eskimo art in Europe . . . and in between, visitors will marvel at the superb collection of Antique Greek ceramics which is the largest of any French museum outside of Paris . . . However, the charm of the buildings remains unspoilt, for a thousand other surprises await at Boulogne Sur Mer's Chateau Museum, Gothic chests, Sevres Porcelain, Renaissance coins, Rodin sculptures, Gallo-Roman and Oceanian objects . . . In all a wonderful history book . . .

FOR FURTHER INFORMATION AND BOOKINGS:

THE CHATEAU MUSEUM
Rue de bernet
62200 BOULOGNE SUR MER
Tél: 21.80.00.80

OPENING TIMES: From May to September:
10 a.m. to 6 p.m. and to
8 p.m. on Fridays.
From October to April:
10 a.m. to 1 p.m. and
2 p.m. to 5 p.m.
Closed on Tuesdays.

DRIVING ON THE RIGHT

For the safety of your passengers, it is important that they are seated in the correct position in the car. In some EC countries it is illegal for children under the age of 7 to sit in the front of the car. In others it is illegal if they are under 12, but whatever the legal requirements, children should *always* sit in the back. In the UK, they should go behind the front passenger, so that they can get into and out of the car from the pavement side, but on the Continent, because you drive on the right, children should sit behind the driver. Child safety locks should be used on both rear doors at all times.

Be very careful when leaving the port; statistics show that if an accident occurs, it will happen within one or two kilometres of the port, or when leaving a garage or other private property. Because the driver may not be familiar with the driving skills required on the Continent, he may not be concentrating fully on the road. Do not be complacent about driving on the right-hand side of the road. There are countless traffic signs, complex junctions, trams, trolleybuses and different priorities to be recognised, understood and complied with, and it is essential to be cautious and vigilant. Plan your driving well and act on both seen and unseen dangers. The following pages will help you understand, recognise and deal with the potential hazards of driving in Europe.

Remember to drive on the right!

3 Driving on the Other Side

OVERTAKE THE PROBLEMS OF DRIVING ABROAD

Have you had the problem of trying to overtake whilst driving on the roads of Europe? Trying to look around that vehicle in front of you, carefully edging out but not having a clear enough view ahead!!

The innovative Summit "Europa" Mirror now allows you to view the road ahead without pulling out towards oncoming traffic and maximises the nearside forward road visibility.

The "Europa's" dual mirror design is fully adjustable to suit all drivers' needs. It is easily installed without the use of tools and can be located on the windscreen by use of fixing bracket.

SUMMIT
EUROPA
m i r r o r

The Summit "Europa" Mirror is a unique concept and stylish design that compliments the interior of any car – a must for anyone driving on the roads of Europe. Suitable for both right and left hand drive vehicles.

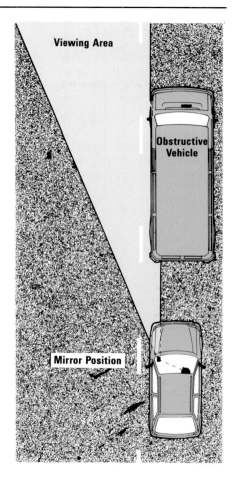

Viewing Area

Obstructive Vehicle

Mirror Position

Summit Accessories Ltd. Unit 6, Wates Way, Wildmere Industrial Estate, Banbury, Oxfordshire OX16 7TS
Tel: 0295 270770 Fax: 0295 270249

ADJUSTMENT OF DRIVING MIRRORS

Because you will be driving on the right-hand side of the road, it is important to pull up somewhere safe to adjust your mirrors before leaving the port. Adjust the interior and nearside exterior mirror (the offside mirror in the UK), and ask a passenger to adjust the offside mirror (unless this can be done electronically).

A good driver will always be aware of the position and speed of any following traffic, and will act sensibly and safely on what he can see. In order to do this, you *must* use the mirrors sensibly and regularly and before signalling, changing direction, slowing down or stopping. One of the most difficult and potentially dangerous manoeuvres for a British driver in Europe is to turn left at an uncontrolled crossroads, and an offside mirror (nearside in the UK) is invaluable. Make sure, therefore, that you have the appropriate mirrors fitted to any vehicle you intend to take on the Continent.

COMPLYING WITH THE LAW

The laws concerning motoring and motoring offences are similar in the majority of EC countries to those in the UK. Because of the forthcoming Single European Market, moreover, laws in Europe are constantly changing. It is, therefore, difficult to

If the mirrors cannot be adjusted electronically from the driver's seat, ask a passenger to help. Adjust your offside mirror so that you can see any vehicle behind you.

quote many specific laws or regulations, but following are some points to be aware of:

- In many European countries there are on-the-spot fines for minor offences, such as exceeding the speed limit. Ensure, therefore, that you are able to pay for these should the need arise.

- Penalties for drinking and driving are a lot more severe in some countries than they are in the UK. Wherever you are, remember that drinking and driving wrecks lives. Just one alcoholic drink can severely affect your driving abilities.

- If you ride a motorbike, you must wear your crash helmet at all times. This will soon be a legal requirement, even for drivers of mopeds.

- It is essential that you always wear your seatbelt, whether you are in the front or back of the car.

- In some countries you may be fined for throwing litter from your car. Always be considerate and dispose of your rubbish properly.

As long as you drive carefully and sensibly, and respect other road users, you should not be breaking the law. For further information on laws relating to specific situations, see pages 59–78.

Wearing a safety helmet is obligatory for motorcyclists.

You must wear a seat belt at all times.

Speed

Your use of speed is an extremely important aspect of your driving anywhere, but particularly abroad where you may encounter totally new driving situations. Avoid using excessive speed in any situation which does not require it. In towns, especially, you should use speed very carefully and approach any potential hazard with caution. Even a simple junction can cause confusion when you are unaccustomed to driving on the right. To give yourself plenty of time to observe and act accordingly, you must reduce your speed.

The following traffic signs show the speed limits on different types of road in eight European countries. For a fuller guide to European speed limits, see the table on page 41.

France.

Belgium.

Denmark.

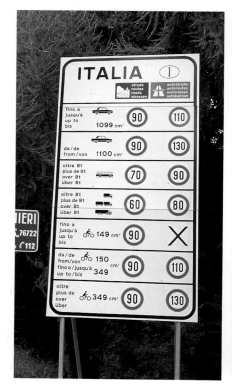

Italy.

Germany.

Netherlands.

EUROPEAN SPEED LIMITS

1 kilometre = 0.62 miles   1 mile = 1.6 kilometres

Switzerland.

Country	Urban roads	Non-urban roads	Motorways
Austria	50 kph	100 kph	130 kph
Belgium	60 kph	90 kph	120 kph
Denmark	50 kph	80 kph	100 kph
Eire	30 mph	55 mph	—
Finland	50 kph	80 kph	120 kph
France	50 kph	90 kph	130 kph
Germany	50 kph	100 kph	130 kph
Greece	40 kph	50 kph	100 kph
Italy	50 kph	90 kph	130 kph
Luxembourg	60 kph	90 kph	120 kph
Netherlands	50 kph	80 kph	120 kph
Norway	50 kph	80 kph	90 kph
Portugal	60 kph	90 kph	120 kph
Spain	40–60 kph	80–100 kph	100–120 kph
Sweden	50 kph	70–80 kph	110 kph
Switzerland	50 kph	80 kph	120 kph

The speed limits given here are accurate guides for each country listed, although you must *always* remain within the speed limit given at the side of the particular road you are on, whatever country it may be in.

To convert kph to mph, simply divide the number of kms by 1.6 to get the mph figure. For example, to convert 80 kph to mph, divide 80 by 1.6 and you should get 50 mph.

LIMITS DE VELOCITAT A LES CARRETERES DE LES VALLS D'ANDORRA

40 PER CIUTAT POR CIUDAD EN VILLE

90 PER CARRETERA POR CARRETERA EN ROUTE

Andorra.

REFUELLING

When planning your holiday, make sure you will have enough fuel. If you run out of fuel on a motorway or in the mountains you may have to wait a long time for a breakdown vehicle to arrive. If you are not insured, the bill may prove very expensive and may, moreover, have to be paid on the spot.

Because fuel prices change so often, it is impossible to quote wholly up-to-date figures, but the table here gives a useful guide. Bear in mind that, although most garages in Europe do accept credit cards, a few may not, so take cash or Eurocheques if possible.

Unleaded fuel is readily available in most EC countries. The table on page 43 lists the correct phrases for leaded, unleaded and diesel fuel in the languages of various European countries, so that you know what to look out for on the pumps when you pull into a petrol station, depending on the type of vehicle you are driving.

FUEL PRICES

Country	Leaded	Unleaded
Austria	211	220
Belgium	248	226
Denmark	279	279
Eire	296	288
Finland	258	238
France	260	246
Germany	256	234
Greece	186	173
Italy	325	312
Luxembourg	180	173
Netherlands	300	276
Norway	294	286
Portugal	275	256
Spain	226	219
Sweden	292	274
Switzerland	203	189

* All prices are in pence per gallon

As you approach the pumps, look for the type of fuel you require.

Country	Leaded	Unleaded	Diesel
Austria	Verbleit	Bleifrei	Diesel
Belgium	Essence Loodvrij	Sans Plomb Super	Diesel
Denmark	Benzin	Blyfri	Diesel
Finland	Normal	Lyijyton	Diesel
France	Essence Plomb	Sans Plomb	Diesel
Germany	Verbleit	Bleifrei	Diesel
Greece	Super Regular	Unleaded	Diesel
Italy	Con Piombo	Senza Piombo	Diesel
Netherlands	Super	Loodvrij	Diesel
Norway	Blyfri	Super	Diesel
Portugal	Gasolina	Sem Chumbo	Gasoleo
Spain	Normal Super Gasolina	Sin Plombo	Diesel
Switzerland			
Lausanne area	Essence Plomb	Sans Plomb	Diesel
Zurich area	Verbleit	Bleifrei	Diesel
Locarno area	Con Piombo	Senza Piombo	Diesel
Sweden	Bensin	Blyfri	Diesel

DRIVING PLANS

A driving plan should be based on three things; what *can* be seen, what *cannot* be seen, and the situation that is likely to develop. It is not enough merely to observe details in a road scene; you must assess every situation, and plan your driving accordingly. Concentration is, of course, essential. The following pictures show an example of a sensible, successful driving plan.

Fog and mist reduce visibility. Slow down so that you can stop in the distance you can see to be clear.

What cannot be seen: If you cannot see whether the road ahead is clear, reduce speed so that you can stop in the distance that you can see is clear.

The circumstances which may reasonably be expected to develop: Unlike the observant pedestrian on the right, who is aware that the traffic signals are about to change, the two younger men are making a dash to beat the tram and signals. Always reduce speed when you approach a crossing – even if you do not see any pedestrians.

TRAFFIC SIGNS AND ROAD MARKINGS

Most of the information provided by traffic signs and road markings is given in symbols rather than words. Signs in Europe are, therefore, usually easy for the British driver to understand and act on. Sometimes, however, signs can be misleading – particularly in large towns, were directions signs can be confusing to a foreigner. It is useful to ask a passenger to navigate whenever possible. If there is no navigator available, it is wise to steer clear of large towns, particularly in rush hours and at other busy periods.

If you concentrate properly, and drive carefully, you should be able to cope with most of the traffic signs in Europe. Following, however, are some examples of the more unusual signs you may see on the Continent. For a further list of European signs, see pages 83–105.

The information signs attached to these railings can only be seen if there is no traffic ahead.

4 Knowing the Signs

Traffic signs in Europe often convey more than one piece of information, so read them carefully.

This sign in Denmark ensures drivers get the message!

You may not understand the language, but the symbol on this sign means the same in any country!

These traffic signals in Luxembourg could confuse a driver. When the part-time traffic lights are working this is a controlled junction. When the lights are not working it becomes an uncontrolled junction, and the STOP sign must be obeyed.

These yellow signs appear everywhere in Europe. They remind drivers that they are on a priority road, and so have the right of way, unless otherwise stated (except at roundabouts).

The sign warns drivers of possible dangers in this narrow cobbled street.

Whenever you enter a town in any country you will see a sign that shows the maximum speed limit. Do not exceed that limit!

The sign in Italy warns drivers that there could be traffic queuing ahead. Perhaps we could do with some of these signs in the UK!

The sign in Denmark reminds drivers to use their headlights. In some countries, motorcyclists are required to keep their lights on at all times.

Drivers may not see the small road on the right, so this sign in Italy is sensibly placed.

It is hardly surprising that this narrow street in Austria is one way!

If you are planning to drive in the mountains, make sure your car is fitted with suitable tyres.

A customs point in Andorra. Stop as indicated, and obey all instructions.

ELECTRONIC TRAFFIC SIGNS AND SIGNALS

Most countries in the EC use electronic traffic signs, and some of the more common examples are given below. Red signs, wherever you are, give orders or warnings; their instructions must always be complied with.

This and the next picture are of the same sign. It warns drivers that the maximum speed limit is 40 kph . . .

. . . and gives the reason for the slow speed limit; there is a sharp double bend in the road ahead.

This amber flashing light warns drivers that a cycle route crosses the road 150 metres ahead.

When the red lights are flashing on this sign, stop! Aircraft will be flying low over the road to land at a nearby airport.

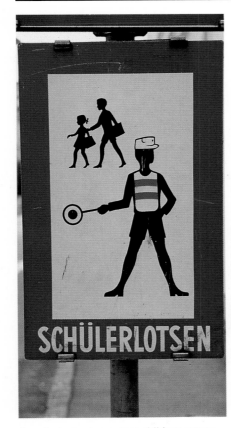

A prefect who supervises children across the road has the same responsibility as a 'lollipop' person in the UK.

Flashing amber lights warn drivers of the pedestrian crossing. The traffic sign informs drivers that children, supervised by a prefect, often use the crossing.

This sign in France warns drivers turning right that pedestrians have priority.

ROAD MARKINGS

Road markings in Europe, like those in the UK, give orders, guidance and warnings. Although they are usually easy for the British driver to understand, there are a few oddities. 'Give Way' signs are often a different shape from those in the UK, and in some countries (for example Austria), road markings are yellow rather than white.

These triangular road markings across the junction mean give way to traffic on the main road.

The arrows on this road in Spain direct traffic to move over to the right. The third lane will merge with the second lane 150 metres ahead.

This picture was taken in Andorra, but the solid white line in the middle of the road means the same in any European country. You must not cross or straddle it except when you need to get in and out of a side road, or when you have to avoid a stationary obstruction.

Cars may not enter this cycle route in Basle, Switzerland.

As in Austria and Switzerland, road markings in Liechtenstein are yellow.

The yellow line on the right of this picture is the outer edge of a cycle route. The sign informs drivers that there is a dangerous exit ahead; hence the change in the road markings in the distance.

This road marking in France informs drivers that they are approaching a school.

The road marking here warns drivers that the road ahead narrows. It's easy to see why!

ROAD JUNCTIONS

One of the most potentially dangerous manoeuvres to perform when driving in the UK is a right turn at a road junction. In Europe, the danger lies in turning left. Whether you approach a 'Y' or 'T' junction, a roundabout, or something even more complicated, you must take the utmost care. Use your mirrors sensibly, and signal your intention to other drivers clearly. Make sure you are in the correct position in the road, and have the most suitable gear.

The following illustrations will show you how to cope with a variety of traffic situations in Europe. Further information about the correct driving procedure to use at road junctions can be found in *The Illustrated Highway Code*, also published by Kogan Page.

Right turn
Taking a right turn is a relatively simple manoeuvre to perform on the Continent compared with in the UK.

When turning right at a crossroads, use your mirrors, slow down, and assess the road situation as early as possible . . .

. . . then indicate, change gear, brake and take the turn.

Make sure it is safe to pull out before doing so. The driver of this car may not have seen the red car approaching, because of the bushes obscuring her view, so she has stopped at the 'Give Way' sign to ensure the road is clear.

Only proceed when you are sure that the way is clear.

Make sure you look carefully in every direction before changing course. Give way to cyclists when you intend to turn right.

In order to turn right at the junction ahead, you will have to cross the tram lines. You must, of course, give way to any trams or trolleybuses.

Left turn

Turning left is one of the most potentially dangerous manoeuvres you will have to perform on the Continent. Drive carefully, and try to gather as much information about the junction you are approaching as possible. What type of junction is it? What is its layout? Are there any traffic signals or road markings? What is the volume of traffic? Are there any tram lines to be crossed? Look well ahead, and formulate a safe driving plan.

When turning left, use your mirrors and assess the situation, then indicate.

Look in your mirrors again, move out to just right of the centre of the road and slow down.

Check in your mirrors once more, then, if it is safe to do so, complete the turn.

The flashing light at this junction in St Tropez informs drivers that they can proceed providing there is no traffic approaching from the right. If there is, however, the driver must wait and let it pass before joining the dual carriageway.

Trams, of course, have right of way. The driver of this coach has not checked properly before turning left, and his mistake may prove fatal.

The road markings at this crossroads in Berlin remind drivers that traffic should pass nearside to nearside when turning left. Any traffic approaching from the right has right of way – hence the 'give way' line.

Roundabouts

Because they are driving on the 'wrong' side of the road, many British drivers find roundabouts in Europe particularly confusing. Until you are used to (and comfortable with) driving conditions on the Continent, you should approach all roundabouts and other complicated junctions very carefully.

A mini roundabout in Luxembourg. Remember – always give way to the left.

This sign in France reminds drivers that they do not have right of way. As you approach the roundabout, check in your mirrors then indicate your intention and slow down.

If you intend to take the third exit on the roundabout (the road leading off to the left), approach the roundabout in the left-hand lane, and stay in that lane until you reach the exit.

This roundabout in Berlin is huge; as you can see from the sign, there are five exits. It is important to ensure that you are in the correct lane as you approach.

As you near your intended exit, indicate clearly, but not too early. Then check carefully all around before moving out into the outside lane.

MOTORWAYS

Today, motorways are the 'arteries' of most European countries. The ease of transport and distribution they provide is fundamental to a country's prosperity, and without them, millions of businesses would grind to a halt. Motorways also, of course, provide advantages to the individual driver. Not only do they cut journey time substantially, they are also, statistically, a very safe method of transport.

There are, however, disadvantages to motorway driving. You will, of course, miss out on seeing much of the country through which you are travelling, and if you have young children in the car they will soon tire of the monotony of the scenery. In some countries, drivers who wish to use the motorway must pay a toll, or motorway tax. How the tax is levied varies from country to country; in Switzerland, for example, all drivers wishing to use the motorway must pay 30 Swiss francs (with an additional 30 francs for caravans or trailers). They are then given a yellow vignette, which should be displayed in the top left corner of the windscreen. These permits are available at border crossings and are valid for multiple re-entry into Switzerland for the duration of the licensed period. To avoid hold-ups at the frontier, however, it is advisable to purchase them from the Swiss National Tourist Office whose address is listed on page 107.

This sign in Italy shows clearly which vehicles are not allowed on the motorway.

Although there is no wording on this sign, it clearly means 'give way'.

Most of the laws relating to motorway driving on the Continent are similar to those in the UK. Pedestrians, animals and certain types of vehicles, for example, are not allowed to use the motorway. There are a few points to bear in mind, though:

- 'Cat's-eyes' are rarely used on the Continent, so pay particular attention to road signs.

- Acceleration lanes on motorways in Europe often have 'Give Way' signs on them. Follow the same procedure as you would in the UK; if there is no gap in the traffic, wait in the acceleration lane until it is safe to join the motorway.

- Direction signs may not be the same colour in every country. Most, like the UK, use blue signs for directions on motorways, but Italy, for example, uses green ones.

The toll booth 1500 metres ahead accepts all major credit cards. If you have the correct change, however, you will save time if you use an 'automatic' ticket booth. Bear in mind that toll booths in Italy do not accept any credit cards at all.

This automatic ticket machine clearly shows the tariffs for different types of vehicles. The ticket you are given will show the place and time of issue. Since you will have to hand the ticket in at the other end, watch your speed – the attendants can work out how fast you travelled!

On the motorway

After joining the motorway, stay in the slow lane until you are used to the driving conditions. Remember – in Europe, traffic will be passing you on your *left*. Use your mirrors regularly so that you are aware of the position of the other traffic on the road, and check your speed. Although motorways in the UK have a speed limit of 70 mph, this varies from country to country on the Continent. See page 41 for a list of speed limits.

This French motorway sign warns drivers that, although the maximum speed limit on the motorway is 130 kph, speed should be reduced to 110 kph in the event of rain.

This is a warning that traffic light signals are working ahead. If you look closely, you will see why!

There are refuges like this on some French roads for drivers who have broken down or need to pull over.

To use this emergency telephone, push down the lever, then wait for the operator to answer your call.

As in the UK, there are emergency telephones for use in case of accident or breakdown on the Continent.

Road works on motorways

Unfortunately, major repairs and resurfacing are as much a fact of life on motorways in the rest of Europe as they are on those in the UK. It would be rare not to encounter some kind of hold-up or diversion on your holiday due to repair work being carried out. One whole side of a carriageway often has to be closed and traffic diverted to the other side to form a contraflow. As in the UK, every precaution should be taken when travelling in a contraflow and any temporary, mandatory or advisory speed limits should be strictly complied with.

You may encounter traffic jams in any country – not just the UK!

Following distance

The excuses given for nose to tail collisions are often ridiculous: 'You braked too hard', 'The road surface must have been slippery', 'Your stop lights don't work', 'The rear of your car came towards me'!

   Make sure you leave ample distance between your car and the one in front. It takes the average driver 0.7 seconds to respond to a sudden situation. In that time the distance travelled would be 30.8 feet for a vehicle travelling at 30 mph (45 kph). To help drivers understand the safe following distance, road markings are given in France which show drivers the correct margin of safety from the vehicle in front. If the road surface is wet, of course, speed should be further reduced, and a greater following distance left.

This sign in France warns drivers of the danger of leaving only one marque's (chevron's) distance between your car and the one in front.

Even in normal conditions, it is essential for safety reasons to leave two marques' following distance.

'Drive, don't race!'

'A fast driver is a dangerous driver!'

Leaving a motorway
Leaving a motorway can be as
dangerous as joining one. Make sure
you know well in advance which exit
you want to take, and position your
vehicle in the nearside lane about
2 kms from the exit.

When you see the countdown marker to
the exit you want, indicate your intentions
and prepare to leave the motorway. Bear in
mind that, whereas in the UK this sign
would mean you are 300 yards from the
exit, on the Continent it means you are
300 metres away.

You will be used to driving faster on the motorway,
so make sure you watch your speed carefully when
you leave it.

TRAMS AND TROLLEYBUSES

Most large cities in Europe have trams and/or trolleybuses as public transport. The position of these vehicles on the road varies from one country to another; some may travel in the middle of the road, and others in the nearside lane.

In some countries buses, like trams, have right of way. In a situation such as this one, therefore, you should give way if the bus is moving off.

The driver of this car is giving way to the tram in Basle, Switzerland. Note that the car is in the correct position on the road for making a left-hand turn.

The driver of this red car must check in his mirrors before turning right. There may be another tram approaching.

PEDESTRIANS

The movements of pedestrians are often unpredictable, and drivers should always be careful – especially when driving through built-up, highly populated areas.

Tourism is a growing industry in many European cities. Pay particular attention, therefore, when driving through a town with a famous tourist attraction. Pedestrian tourists will be as unused to European road systems as you are, and may be concentrating on sightseeing rather than the road!

Take care, too, when driving past tram stops, schools, and other places where you may find a lot of pedestrians.

Some countries, for example Germany, have a law against jay-walking. In this picture in Madrid pedestrians can be seen crossing the road despite the green traffic light signal. However annoyed you may be, you must slow down and allow them to cross.

Just as a good driver will always be sensitive to the safety and needs of pedestrians, so should you respect drivers if you are on foot. The different traffic conditions on the Continent affect pedestrians as well as drivers. Remember to look *left* as well as right, for example, when crossing the road. If you encounter a pelican crossing, make sure you obey the signals shown – even if the road seems clear. In some countries (for example Germany) you can be fined for crossing when the lights are red.

Always cross the road using a subway or a pelican crossing if there is one available.

OVERTAKING

Overtaking should be achieved in the shortest possible time and distance, and without causing any inconvenience or danger to other traffic. Make sure, when you overtake, that you are complying with lane restrictions and speed limits. If you are driving your own car in Europe, your reduced visibility is a severe disadvantage. Your steering wheel is, of course, located on the right-hand side of the car, yet you will also be driving on the right, and so will have a reduced view of oncoming traffic. To counter this, you should get into a position to overtake earlier than you would do in the UK. This will improve your view of the road ahead, but reduce the view to the nearside (see figure 2B). Do not ask your passenger when it is safe to pull out even though they may have a better view of oncoming traffic than you. Always trust your own judgement rather than theirs (see Figure 2A).

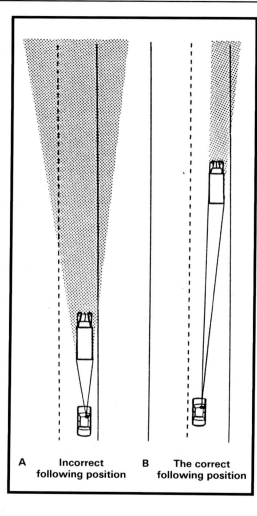

A   **Incorrect following position**

B   **The correct following position**

Before you overtake, you should assess:

- the speed of the vehicle(s) to be overtaken;

- the speed and performance of your own vehicle;

- the speed and distance of any approaching vehicle which is in, or could come into view;

- the distance to be covered while overtaking;

- whether you really need to overtake.

Figure 2   *Correct (A) and incorrect (B) following positions when driving on the right in a right-hand drive vehicle.*

PARKING AND LEAVING THE VEHICLE

Parking laws and restrictions vary from country to country, but wherever you park, you must make sure that you are not causing an obstruction.

Before leaving your vehicle unattended you should:

- remove the ignition key (and activate the steering lock if you have one);
- close all windows;
- lock the boot, sunroof and all the doors;
- put any valuables out of sight (preferably in the boot).

If you are travelling in a hot country, it is a good idea to cover the windscreen, so that the car is not too hot on your return.

Do not park your vehicle at a bus stop.

This driver in Madrid is getting a ticket for parking illegally!

Do not park your vehicle on a cycle path.

MOUNTAINS

Europe's mountain ranges are a breathtaking sight. They are also potentially very dangerous and, particularly in winter with adverse weather conditions, can prove extremely hazardous to the motorist. Find out about weather conditions *before* you set out, and contact the tourist board to check that mountain passes are open (some are closed in winter). Take extra care on the winding mountain roads – visibility will be poor, particularly if there is low cloud.

Low cloud on mountains will drastically reduce visibility.

Descending a mountain

Descending a mountain can be a nerve-racking experience for drivers! The following guidelines show how to reach the bottom as safely as possible.

- Controlled, progressive braking is essential – do not brake too hard or suddenly.

- Maintain a long stopping distance throughout your descent. Remember, the recommended stopping distance for cars on a level, dry road will not apply to a car driving down a 1 in 5 gradient!

- Keep in a low gear, and use this low gear as a back-up for your brakes.

- Adjust your brake pressure according to the condition of the road surface. Gravel, cobbles, tarmac etc all affect tyre adhesion in different ways.

- Brake firmly on straight sections of the road, and ease off the brake as you approach bends.

The view may be awesome, but drivers must concentrate on the road, not on the scenery!

Drive carefully around hairpin bends.

Coaches should be given priority on mountain roads. Their poor manoeuvrability makes it hard for their drivers to negotiate hairpin bends and, in some countries, coaches have automatic right of way on winding mountain roads.

To overtake in such a dangerous place is extremely foolish.

Look across hairpin bends to check for oncoming traffic, and give way to any coaches.

Tunnels

Some mountains (for example Mont Blanc) have tunnels through them, and this spares drivers time in driving over them. As you approach a tunnel, switch your headlights on, and remember that once inside the tunnel it is an offense to:

- reverse;

- do a 'U'-turn;

- overtake another vehicle (unless there is a dual carriageway);

- stop, unless there is an emergency or a breakdown. (See page 78 for further information about breakdowns.)

This tunnel in Spain would not be high enough for some vehicles. There are also no lights in the tunnel and so headlights are essential!

Switch your lights on before entering the tunnel.

LEVEL CROSSINGS

Level crossings on the Continent are similar to those in the UK. Approach them with care, and obey all the warning instructions. *Never* drive nose-to-tail over a level crossing, and do not linger! Above all, if the warning sounds while you are actually on the crossing, *do not panic*. You will have plenty of time to cross, as long as you drive carefully and sensibly.

If you do break down on the crossing, or if you think that there is a problem, use the emergency telephone to contact the signalman.

This sign painted on the road in Italy is a warning that there is a level crossing ahead.

This level crossing warning sign in France is similar to those found in the UK.

ROAD SURFACES

Because of the different climates and landscapes, there is a wider variety of road surfaces on the Continent than there is in the UK. Some may become dangerous in extreme conditions; cobbles, for example, can get very slippery when wet. Take extra care, therefore, when you see a change in the road surface. Slow down, and moderate your driving to suit the new conditions.

This road surface in Spain is loose gravel and dust; in wet conditions it could be dangerous.

BREAKDOWNS

In the event of a breakdown or puncture, it is important to get the vehicle off the road if possible. If you cannot, make sure your passengers leave the vehicle and get clear of the road. Then, warn other road users of the obstruction. Use your hazard warning lights if they are fitted, and your sidelights, too, if visibility is poor. Place a warning triangle on the road, at least 50 metres from the vehicle (150 metres on the hard shoulder of a motorway). If you need to take anything from the boot of the vehicle, take care not to hide the warning lamps from approaching traffic.

If anything falls from your vehicle, stop as soon as possible and display the warning lights, the sidelights and the warning triangle. Then remove whatever has fallen from the car from the carriageway.

Should you break down or drop something on the motorway, the above procedure does *not* apply. Instead, pull over on to the hard shoulder, and contact the police using the emergency telephone. Both the AA and the RAC offer a breakdown protection policy for drivers on holiday in Europe. For further details, contact them at the addresses given on page 110.

The minimum distance required by law is 50 metres before the hazard. A warning triangle must not be used as an excuse for illegal parking or stopping.

It is both illegal and irresponsible to place your warning triangle so close to the car in the event of a breakdown.

ENJOY THE FREEDOM OF MOTORING ON THE CONTINENT WITH FREE EUROPEAN BREAKDOWN COVER

If you're planning a motoring or business holiday we think a little foresight in joining National Breakdown could save you a small fortune with **free European cover**.

Imagine breaking down whilst motoring on the Continent. Who would you turn to for help?

You could be miles from anywhere. That's why it's important to have breakdown protection abroad.

When you're a member of National Breakdown you can rest assured one free phone call will bring fast expert help no matter where you are in Europe, no matter who's driving at the time of the breakdown or accident.

With fully computerised control centres in the UK and Strasbourg and a European network of over 6,000 agents on-call 24 hours a day, you can drive across the Continent with confidence.

There are four excellent value schemes to choose from, so you're sure to find one to suit your needs.

And if you take out one of our top levels of cover, either Total Protection or Comprehensive from this advertisement you'll find European Cover is absolutely FREE, so there's no need to purchase separate cover.

That's not all, National Breakdown provide a variety of other services to help you when travelling in Europe. For starters there's a European brochure available which gives full details of travelling abroad including ferry sailings.

Then there's our Blue Riband service which offers you additional Medical Expenses for you and your passengers, plus a FREE Camping Carnet. And if you're going by ferry, National Breakdown can save you time and trouble by arranging your booking for you.

Don't worry if you're a member of another motoring organisation, simply let us know when your current cover expires and we'll do the rest.

Last year, National Breakdown helped thousands of motorists holidaying abroad, so don't waste another minute. Call us now to join, or for more information clip the coupon and return to us.

National Breakdown, FREEPOST, Leeds LS99 2NB.

CALL FREE ☎ 0800 800 600

National Breakdown is a member of the Green Flag Group of Companies

Certificate Nº FS13808

At your service for half the price !

Bodywork repair

servicing

Courtesy car : 4£/a day *
Go shopping while we work

Parts & **equipments**
Genuine parts, alarm, tow bar...

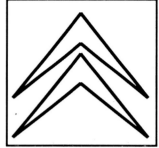

Official Main Dealer
All Works are fully guaranted **

easy to cross, easy to find, easy to save

Boulogne / mer - *L I A N E automobiles*

Follow indicators " Z. I. de la Liane " along the riverside, direction : N1 - Abbeville - Le Touquet - 3 mn from the port

Visa & Amex Card, Travellers Check wellcome

from UK, Dial first **010 + 33 + 21 99 21 11 - Fax : 21 92 46 81**
WORKSHOP : 21 99 21 12 open non stop MON to SAT, from 7.30am to 6.30pm
Parts & equipments : 21 99 21 15 Please, Phone or Fax for return quotation !

english spoken . Call or Fax for an appointment !

* Citroën AX saloon, 2 seaters, can be booked for 4 £ a day, during the works. Insurance included. ** return détails on request

COMING HOME

Your homeward journey will be similar to your outward journey (but not as exciting). Follow the procedures that you have learnt so far, and drive sensibly and carefully.

Remember – good driving need not be a chore. With practice and patience, driving on the Continent can be a great pleasure, and is guaranteed to enhance your holidays.

Goodbye, and safe driving!

Ah! to B&Ireland
(at the end of a perfect day)

We're the Irish owned travel company that offers convenient comfortable and competitively priced ferry routes from Holyhead to the heart of Dublin and from Pembroke to Rosslare.

B&I offers great family value saving pounds on fares and on board in our duty free shops and restaurants. We also have the most extensive range of inclusive holidays in Ireland by both sea and air.

Get the B&I Holidays in Ireland brochure now by calling 051-236 8325.

Holiday B&Ireland
THE IRISH EXPERTS

**HOLYHEAD – DUBLIN
PEMBROKE – ROSSLARE**

B&I LINE

A country-by-country selection of
some common European traffic signs.

ANDORRA

Barrier in 50 metres

AUSTRIA

School crossing in 100 metres

Possible traffic jams ahead

Dangerous exit in 100 metres

BELGIUM

Except for emergency and service vehicles

No sliproad

Restrictions still apply

DENMARK

Road markings missing

Wet, slippery road surface

No overtaking by trucks, buses and cars with trailers

FRANCE

Six tonne limit, no caravans, right of way to pedestrians. Parking prohibited

Frequent fog

Height restriction of 4.1 metres for the next 7 kms

Give way at junction

Priority held by vehicles from the left at this roundabout

Warning of vehicles leaving a factory exit ahead

GERMANY

Keep your distance using the markings

Beware! Steps/ditches in the road

Children's play area, children crossing

Damaged roads

Bus lane (for scheduled traffic only)

ITALY

Falling rocks

For the next 2 kms the valley side of the road has
no barriers

Traffic forbidden in this zone except taxis, bicycles
and vehicles for the disabled

Cars manoeuvring/pulling out

Right-hand lane reserved for buses and taxis only

LUXEMBOURG

Roadworks ahead, no overtaking, 40 kph speed limit

Litterbugs will be prosecuted

THE NETHERLANDS

Cyclists

School crossing in 1300 metres

Ridge in the road

Except for loading and unloading

SPAIN

Dangerous crossing ahead. 60 kph limit

Crawler lane on the right. 60 kph limit on the left

60 kph limit. Speed controlled by radar
(ie a speed trap)

Pedestrians should walk on the left-hand
side of the road

Diversion in 500 metres

SWITZERLAND

No access to pedestrians or agricultural vehicles

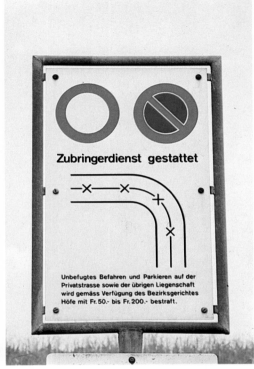

Delivery vehicles only

TOURIST OFFICES

The following tourist offices should be able to provide you with any information or guidance you will need for your holiday.

Austrian National Tourist Office
30 St George St
London W1R 0AL
Tel: 071-629 0461
Fax: 071-499 6038

Belgian Tourist Office
Premier House
2 Gayton Way
Harrow
Middx
Tel: 081-861 3300
Fax: 081-427 6760

Danish Tourist Board
PO Box 2LT
London W1A 2LT
Tel: 071-734 2637
Fax: 071-494 2170

Dutch Tourist Office
25–28 Buckingham Gate
London SW1E 6LD
Tel: 071-630 0451
Fax: 071-828 7941

Finnish Tourist Board
66–68 Haymarket
London SW1Y 4RF
Tel: 071-839 4048
Fax: 071-321 0696

French National Tourist Board
178 Piccadilly
London W1J 0AI
Tel: 071-499 6911/7622
Fax: 071-493 6594

German National Tourist Office
Nightingale House
65 Curzon Street
London W1Y 7PE
Tel: 071-495 3990
Fax: 071-495 6129

Greek Tourist Office
4 Conduit Street
London W1R 0DJ
Tel: 071-734 5997
Fax: 071-287 1369

Italian Tourist Office
1 Princess Street
London W1R 8AY
Tel: 071-408 1254
Fax: 071-493 6695

Luxembourg Tourist Office
36–37 Piccadilly
London W1V 9PA
Tel: 071-434 2800
Fax: 071-734 1205

Norwegian Tourist Office
Charles House
5–11 Lower Regent Street
London SW1Y 4LR
Tel: 071-839 6255
Fax: 071-893 6014

Portuguese Tourist Office
22–25A Sackville Street
London W1X 1DE
Tel: 071-494 1441
Fax: 071-494 18688

Spanish Tourist Office
57–58 James Street
London SW1A 1LD
Tel: 071-499 0901
Fax: 071-629 4257

Swedish Tourist Office
29–31 Oxford Street
London W1R 1RE
Tel: 071-437 5816
Fax: 071-287 0164

Swiss National Tourist Office
Swiss Centre
New Coventry Street
London W1V 8EE
Tel: 071-734 1921
Fax: 071-437 4577

Useful Addresses

FERRY PORTS AND OPERATORS

The following will enable you to contact a variety of ports and ferry operators for the information you require. You can then select which are best for your travel (and financial) plans and make a reservation.

Dover
To Boulogne and Calais
Sealink
Central Reservations
Charter House
Park Street
Ashford
Kent TN24 8EX
Tel: 0233 646024

Hoverspeed
Maybrook House
Queens Gardens
Dover
Kent CT17 9UQ
Tel: 0304 240241

Felixstowe
To Zeebrugge
P&O European Ferries
Channel House
Channel View Road
Dover
Kent CT17 9TJ
Tel: 081-575 8555

Folkstone
To Boulogne
Sealink – *see* Dover

Harwich
To Scandinavia and Germany
Scandinavian Seaways
Scandinavia House
Parkeston Quayway
Harwich
Essex CO12 4QE
Tel: 0255 508122

Newhaven
To Dieppe
Sealink – *see* Dover

Portsmouth
To Jersey and Guernsey
British Channel Island Ferries
PO Box 315
Poole
Dorset BH15 4DB
Tel: 0202 681155

Ramsgate
To Dunkirk
Sally Line
81 Piccadilly
London WV1F 9HF
Tel: 0843 595522

Hollyhead
To Dun Laoghaire
B&I Line
Reliant House
Water Street
Liverpool L2 8TP
Tel: 051-227 3131

Some ferry companies, such as P&O and Sealink, run services from a number of different ports to a variety of destinations. Simply give them a call and ask them to send you a brochure detailing all their services to the Continent.

BRITISH EMBASSIES IN EUROPE

British Embassies and Consulates can be contacted in case of emergencies.

Austria
British Embassy
Jauresgàsse 12
1030 Vienna
Tel: (222) 7131575/9
Fax: (222) 757824

Belgium
British Embassy
Britannia House
rue Joseph II 28
1040 Brussels
Tel: (02) 2179000
Fax: (02) 2176763

Denmark
British Embassy
Kastelsvej 36/38/40
DK 2100 Copenhagen
Tel: (31) 26 4600
Fax: (31) 381012

Finland
British Embassy
16–20 Undenmeankaki
00120 Helsinki 12
Tel: (0) 647922
Fax: (0) 611747

France
British Embassy
35 rue du Fauborg St Honoré
75383 Paris
Cedex 08
Tel: (1) 42 66 91 42
Fax: (1) 42 66 95 90

British Consulate
c/o P&O European Ferries
41 Place d'Armes
62100 Calais Cedex
Tel: (21) 263376
Fax: (21) 969757

Germany
British Embassy
Friedrich-Ebert-Allée 77
5300 Bonn 1
Tel: (228) 234061
Fax: (228) 234070

British Embassy
Olympia Stadion
1000 Berlin 19
Tel: (30) 305 3091
Fax: (30) 305 0197

Greece
British Embassy
1 Ploutarchou St
106 75 Athens
Tel: (01) 7236211
Fax: (01) 7241872

British Consultate
2 Alexandras Avenue
49100 Corfu
Tel: 0661 30 055
Fax: 0661 37995

Republic of Ireland
British Embassy
31/33 Merrion Road
Dublin 4
Tel: 695211
Fax: 838423

Italy
British Embassy
Via XX Septembre 80A
00187 Roma
Tel: (06) 626119
Fax: (06) 474 1836

British Consulate General
Via San Paolo 7
20121 Milan
Tel: (02) 8693442
Fax: (02) 72020153

Luxembourg
British Embassy
14 Boulevard Roosevelt PO Box 874
L-2018 Luxembourg Ville
Tel: 29864/66
Fax: 29867

The Netherlands
British Embassy
Lang Voorhout 10
2514 ED
The Hague
Tel: (30) 364 5800
Fax: (30) 70603839

British Consulate General
Koningslaan 44
1074 AE
Amsterdam
Tel: (20) 764343
Fax: (20) 761069

Norway
British Embassy
Thomas Heftyesgate 8
0244 Oslo 2
Tel: (02) 55 24 00
Fax: (02) 55 10 41

Portugal
British Embassy
35–37 Rua de S Domingo à Lapa
37 1200 Lisbon Cedex
Tel: (01) 3961191
Fax: (01) 626768

Spain
British Embassy
Calle de Fernando del Santo 16
Madrid 4
Tel: (01) 319 0200
Fax: (01) 319 0423

British Consulate
Plaza Nueva 8 (Dpdo)
41001 Seville
Tel: 228875
Fax: 228874

Sweden
British Embassy
Skarpögatan 6–8
115 27 Stockholm
Tel: (08) 6670140
Fax: (08) 66 29989

Switzerland
British Embassy
Thunstrasse 50
3005 Berne 15
Tel: (31) 445021/6
Fax: (31) 440583

ASSOCIATIONS AND CLUBS

Automobile Association
Fanum House
Basingstoke
Hampshire
RG21 2EA
Tel: 0256 20123

The Camping and Caravanning Club
Greenfields House
Westwood Way
Coventry
CV4 8JN
Tel: 0203 694995

The Caravan Club
East Grinstead House
East Grinstead
West Sussex
RH19 1ZB
Tel: 0342 326944

Royal Automobile Club
RAC House
PO Box 100
Lansdowne Road
Croydon
CR9 2JA
Tel: 081 686 2525

Royal Yachting Association
RYA House
Romsey Road
Eastleigh
Hampshire
SO5 4YA
Tel: 0703 629962

Road atlases

Michelin, George Philip, Bartholomew, Collins, the RAC, the AA and others all publish good large scale atlases for Europe. Atlases for more specific regions are also available. These include:

AA Road Maps of Europe series
European Road Maps series, RAC
Motoring Atlas of France, RAC
Paris Street Map, RAC
Regional Maps of France series, RAC

Guide books

Additionally, there are several travel guides to European countries and cities, some including details of tour routes, hotels and restaurants. These include:

The Back Roads of France,
    Bartholomew
Berlitz Travel Guides series
Baedecker maps, tour guides and city
    guides, AA
Fodor Travel Guides
Michelin Red Guides series
RAC European Motoring Guide
RAC Travel Guides
Rough Guides
Touring in Europe by Michael Spring,
    Fodor

Recommended Maps and Guides

Index of Advertisers